JAZZ

An Introduction to its Musical Basis

JAZZ

An Introduction to its Musical Basis

AVRIL DANKWORTH

LONDON

OXFORD UNIVERSITY PRESS

NEW YORK   TORONTO

Oxford University Press, Walton Street, Oxford OX2 6DP

OXFORD LONDON GLASGOW NEW YORK
TORONTO MELBOURNE WELLINGTON CAPE TOWN
IBADAN NAIROBI DAR ES SALAAM TOKYO
KUALA LUMPUR SINGAPORE JAKARTA HONG KONG
DELHI BOMBAY CALCUTTA MADRAS KARACHI

ISBN 0 19 316501 5

© Oxford University Press 1968

First Published 1968
Reprinted 1969, 1972, 1975
and 1979

Printed in Great Britain

Acknowledgements are due to the following for permission to reproduce extracts from songs or music: Chappell & Co. Inc. (*All the Things You Are* — Copyright 1939); Cromwell Music Ltd. (*Take This Hammer*); Herman Darewski Music Publishing Co. (*Sugarfoot Stomp* [*Dippermouth Blues*]); Sam Fox Publishing Co. (London) Ltd. (*You Turned the Tables on Me*); Gershwin Publishing Corporation (*There's a Boat that's Leaving Soon For New York* — Copyright 1935); Kensington Music Ltd. (*Django*); Leeds Music Ltd. (*Cornet Chop Suey*); Peter Maurice Music Co. Ltd. (*Honky Tonk Train Blues*); Melrose Music Corporation (*Sugarfoot Stomp* [*Dippermouth Blues*]); Melrose Bros. Music Co. Inc. (*Frog Legs Rag* — Copyright 1906/1930); Mills Music Ltd. (*East St. Louis Toodle-oo*); Robbins Music Corporation Ltd. (*Panama*); Philips Records Ltd (transcription from recordings of *East St. Louis Toodle-oo* and *Dippermouth Blues*); HMV (transcription from recording of *Let's Pretend that There's a Moon*); Decca Record Co. Ltd. (transcription from recordings of *Panama* and *All the Things You Are*).

Foreword

To the average teenager, pop music and jazz are two quite distinct forms of music. But to adults the difference is not always so clear; certain musicians scorn what *they* describe as jazz, when it is pretty clear that they are really referring to pop. In this way they show their ignorance of an important branch of twentieth-century music.

In fact, pop music has only the slenderest direct connection with jazz. Pop music is popular. It is the 'music of the people': songs and dance tunes calculated to tickle the ear and touch the pocket of the masses, churned out through radio, television, films, and recordings. Each melody is a five-minute wonder—pop tunes rarely last much more than six weeks, though every now and then one does survive and becomes a 'standard'.

Jazz is not for the masses: it is a minority interest—just like 'classical' music. It is a specific kind of music, which operates within quite strict rules. It is also by nature an improvisatory art, almost alone among music of this century. And it implies a feeling, a style—to understand it one must be familiar with its lilt and idiom, which is caught rather than taught. In all these ways it is something special, different from other sorts of music, and with a character of its own.

In this book, I have tried to outline briefly the musical bases of jazz—the forms, the harmonies, the melodies, the instrumentations —to show what they are, and how they have changed from one period to another. This is not a history of jazz, though naturally the historical background is mentioned from time to time: there are enough books already which tell the story of jazz and jazz personalities. Instead, I have written something for the ordinary musical reader, for music students, and teachers of music in schools. Jazz only came into existence seventy years ago, but it has rapidly established itself as a genuine branch of music, and it enjoys worldwide appreciation. Everyone interested in music ought at least to try and understand something of its nature.

Eras and Events in the History of Jazz

Before 1865	Period of Negro slavery. Their music mainly: (a) Work Songs, (b) Blues, (c) Gospel Songs and Spirituals.
1865	Civil War ended. Slavery legally abolished.
1865–90	Transitional period. Development of Negro music, especially in big cities, e.g. New Orleans.
1890s and 1900s	Ragtime style of piano playing widely popular throughout America and elsewhere. Sophisticated City Blues performed by theatre singers. Instrumental groups in demand for all social occasions; small-group improvised music.
1910s and 1920s	Period of 'Traditional' Negro Jazz. Negro players began to move to other cities, especially Chicago.
1920s	Chicago era. Traditional Negro jazz continued to develop. 'Chicago' jazz—an adaptation of New Orleans style by white musicians living in Chicago at the time.
1930s	Development of Swing. Bigger bands necessitated the writing down of jazz (arranging) as a background for improvised solos.
Late 1930s	'Revivalist' movement reacted against this.
1940s	Bebop: New small-group improvisation incorporating harmonic, rhythmic, and melodic innovations.

| 1950s | Cool Jazz : Best of Bop experiments blended with a more 'legitimate' style of playing. East and West Coast Schools. Thirdstream music appeared. |
| 1960s | Experiments in twentieth century non-jazz techniques; modal, atonal, and twelve-note methods. |

Contents

PART ONE

GENERAL MUSICAL FEATURES

Introductory

Most jazz is in the form of melodic and rhythmic variations upon a theme. The theme is usually a twelve-bar blues melody, the chorus of a popular dance-tune, or a specially composed theme. The basic form is usually simple, with square-cut four- or eight-bar phrases.

There is often a short introduction; then the theme is played by the entire group—combo or band ('combo' is the term for a small combination of players)—followed by a series of variations known as 'choruses'. The first chorus is often pretty close to the theme, only slightly decorated; but with each successive chorus comes further embellishment of melody and rhythm, according to the inspiration, desire, and skill of the player. The more the embellishment, the less obvious is the relationship of the variation to the first statement of the theme: the later choruses often break away from it entirely and become new melodies over the existing harmonies. The final variation, as in 'classical' music, either recaptures the clear-cut spirit of the opening as a final reminder of the original, or works up to an exciting coda or summing-up of all that has gone before.

The improvisation may be solo or collective. When a soloist improvises, he is free to do as he pleases, while the other players combine to accompany him in a harmonic-rhythmic background. But in many performances there are times when everyone improvises simultaneously; this is called collective or group improvisation ('jam sessions'), and here, obviously, each player carries the responsibility of disciplining himself to become part of the whole, and not playing in a way that is conspicuous. The result is a kind of polyphony: only the rhythm section maintains the steady harmonic-rhythmic beat, while the melodic instruments improvise in counterpoint above it. Since they all work on the same harmonic progressions everything fits—or should fit!—together.

A 'break' is a small cadenza which occurs at the end of a phrase with a long note or rest, at which point the soloist is left high and dry without the support of the other instruments. A 'riff' is a short phrase—usually of two or four bars—many times repeated over the changing harmonies of the theme. Greatly favoured as a device for accompaniment, especially during the Swing era, it may also be used by an instrumentalist in the course of his solo.

On the whole, traditional (New Orleans) jazz favours collective improvisation, but in music of the Swing era and since, solo variations have held prime place. Further, traditional jazz is entirely spontaneous, each musician working without music—'ad-libbing' in musicians' language. But since the late twenties, much of the collective work and accompaniment of swing, bop, and modern jazz have been 'arranged'—that is, written down in improvisatory style. In this case, the soloist has a prepared background over which he works. 'Composition'—except for some modern works—usually implies the 'theme' upon which the variations are built. The musician who writes down variations upon this theme is known as the 'arranger'.

1. Chords

First, we consider the chords over which the jazzman improvises. In the beginning the Negroes took the harmony of the music they heard around them and adapted it to their own use to harmonize blues, stomps, and so on. This music consisted of popular dance-music of European origin, largely French and Spanish—the polka, quadrille, habañera, tango: popular American music—the cake-walk and minstrel songs; military music; light classical music; and evangelical hymns. All these were based on a simple harmonic system centred mainly on three chords, tonic, subdominant, and dominant. The Negroes took these chords, combining them with their own melodies and rhythms, adding new notes, and placing them in new relationships with each other.

In turn, these harmonized blues and stomps became the basis of jazz improvisation; popular non-Negro dances of the day were also used for the same purpose. It must be constantly borne in mind that jazz is a *way of playing* material which already exists. The jazz musician must commit to memory the chord-progressions of a number, then proceed to extemporize variations upon it. The chord-sequence is the skeleton; the melody the flesh; and variations the clothing.

Over the years jazz (like classical music) has increased the harmonic excitement by adding new notes and colours to the basic diatonic harmony and developing the possibilities of modulation. In New Orleans jazz and swing the harmonies may be decorated, and occasional chords changed from the original blues[1] or dance tune, but substantially the chord sequence is taken *en bloc*. In modern jazz, however, the arranger may choose to re-harmonize a number completely, perhaps with more chromaticism and modulation, this new harmony being established in the first statement of the theme.

During the twenties, contemporary popular material was used,

[1] For standard harmonization of the blues, see p. 48.

but since then jazz musicians have often used popular tunes of earlier decades as well as contemporary numbers. During and since the fifties, more jazz musicians than ever before compose their own themes for variation, possibly because contemporary songs do not give sufficient harmonic scope. Songs from the shows and ballads are used, but pop songs are usually very limited in their harmonic range.

In jazz and popular music the technical name for each chord is rarely used, but is replaced by the actual lettername of the root of the chord; in notation this is indicated by a chord-symbol. The chord-symbols are devised for easy reading. But they also make for easy comprehension of the chord-system: those familiar with simple diatonic harmony up to the dominant seventh have only to link their knowledge with the practical chord-symbol system to find that they have short-circuited much of the laborious business involved in studying 'chromatic harmony' from a textbook. For instance the four types of chord—major, minor, diminished, and augmented— and three chords of the seventh built on the note C, are described as follows:

In chord-symbols the term 'minor' applies to the third of the chord; otherwise the chord is understood to be major. The term 'major' applies to the seventh; otherwise the seventh is understood to be minor.

Almost any combination of sounds may be represented in some way by a chord-symbol. Chord progressions for piano and guitar are written as follows:

$$G_7 \quad / \quad / \quad / \quad C \quad / \quad C_7 \quad /$$

Often a soloist has to improvise over a harmonic progression set out in this way. In Howard Brubeck's 'Dialogue for Jazz Combo and Symphony Orchestra' musical notation is almost absent in the jazz parts, the notation being simply a chord sequence written in the 'chord symbol' system.

The tunes listed on p. 81, composed over four decades, show the sort of numbers used as the basis of jazz improvisation. A glance at the keys shows that: (a) mostly major keys are used, (b) flat keys are favoured more than sharp, (c) there are few key signatures with more than four flats (two exceptions: 'Frogs Legs Rag' and 'Django').

DIATONIC CHORDS

The harmony of most popular songs is pretty firmly centred round the three primary triads—tonic, subdominant, and dominant; the first two of these may appear with an added sixth—that is, the major sixth from the root:

Of the secondary triads, the mediant chord is little used in popular music; the leading-note chord is rarely used either, and even then it usually has an added diatonic seventh; likewise the supertonic and submediant chords.

In tunes of the twenties modulation is almost entirely limited to the nearly related keys, but since 1939 there has been more extensive modulation, taking the ear further away from the diatonic centre.

Four-, five-, and six-note chords are built by adding further thirds to the basic triad. A favourite four-note chord, probably the most used in popular music and jazz, is that of the 'seventh', sometimes known as the 'normal seventh'. This is a chord built on the same plan as the dominant seventh—that is, a major chord plus the minor seventh from the root. The seventh on C is indicated by the chord-symbol: 'C₇' (see p. 4) Any other chord using a seventh in its formation is described similarly. For example: 'C min 7' indicates the chord of C minor plus the minor seventh from the root. 'C maj 7' indicates the C major chord plus the major seventh from the root.

Of the primary triads, now and again the tonic and subdominant triads appear with an added diatonic (major) seventh. In all periods the dominant chord appears almost consistently with the added diatonic seventh. During and since the thirties it also appears with the added ninth, eleventh, and thirteenth; of these forms, the ninth is the most popular:

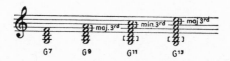

All added notes are in the major diatonic scale of the root except the seventh, which is normally minor.

The following Gershwin extract shows the dominant seventh with the diatonic ninth and eleventh added:

'There's a boat that's leaving soon for New York' (bars 1–3).
Published 1935

✕ *Dominant seventh with added ninth and eleventh*

This could have been harmonized as:

but the B flat and G are used to decorate dominant harmony.

In tunes of the twenties a number of secondary triads have an added diatonic seventh; the supertonic chord is used considerably and often has the seventh added. During the thirties an even larger proportion of secondary triads add the seventh, and since the forties, supertonic, mediant, and submediant chords rarely appear without it. In each case the resulting chord is virtually a 'normal' seventh with a flattened third; as in bars 1 and 2 of the following:

'All the things you are' (bars 1–4). Published 1940

× *Chords with added diatonic seventh*

CHROMATIC CHORDS

When any note of a diatonic chord is inflected in any way, the chord becomes chromatic even if its *root* is diatonic. The harmonies of 'standards' upon which jazz is based show—over five decades—a gradual increase in the amount of chromaticism used. Not that tunes of the twenties are by any means limited to 'hymn-tune' harmonies; far from it; although they are firmly rooted diatonically *around* the primary triads, a quite surprising number of chromatic notes of one kind or another are used.

The publishing of Jerome Kern's 'All the things you are' in 1939 seemed to set the pattern for wider experiments in harmonic possibilities; the harmonies of this song 'kaleidoscope' from one chromatic chord to another, making extensive use of seventh chords—'normal' and otherwise. The early bop experimenters grabbed this Kern number as an admirable vehicle for improvisation because of its harmonic freedom; perhaps it is because few popular songs offer such opportunities that modern jazzmen started more frequently composing their own themes; for example, 'Django' and 'Grass Point'. A popular song of the fifties favoured by modern jazz improvisers is 'How High the Moon'.

When standards of the past are used, they are the ones which offer harmonic scope to the improviser within the framework of their existing harmonic progression. For example, 'Body and Soul' from the thirties is a favourite with the modernists.

To produce 'normal' seventh chords on any note of the major scale other than the dominant involves the use of chromatic notes (notes not belonging to the diatonic scale):

These are all chromatic chords in the key of C, for although the root of each chord belongs to the scale of C major, all the notes of the chords themselves do not. In four cases (II, III, VI, VII) the basic triad (minor or diminished) has been changed to become major. In two cases (I, IV) the diatonic major seventh from the root has been changed to become minor. These chords may merely decorate the original diatonic triad or serve the purpose of modulation, transitory or otherwise.

'Cornet Chop Suey' (bars 9–12)

×*Chord of the seventh on Tonic (diatonic root)*

A device which became popular in the twenties and has remained so is the use of strings of sevenths as a cycle with their roots descending in fifths.

'Panama' (Section A, bars 28–31). Published 1911

The only time that dominant harmony becomes chromatic is when the diatonic ninth, eleventh, or thirteenth is inflected.

'Panama' (Section B, bars 5–8)

×*Dominant seventh with altered ninth ·*

Composers of the twenties seem to show a predilection for major chords, and chords of the normal seventh are widely used, outweighing by far the use of other sevenths. In the list on p. 81, of the nine pieces representing the twenties, seven use the seventh or ninth on the tonic and seven the seventh on the submediant; these two particular chords have not been favoured much since. However, the seventh and ninth on the supertonic was a much-used chord during the twenties which has continued to be used widely.

'Let's pretend that there's a moon' (bars 23–24). Published 1934

×Seventh on Supertonic (diatonic root)

Copyright 1934 by Harms Inc., used by permission.

CHORDS BUILT ON CHROMATIC DEGREES OF THE SCALE

Normal sevenths built upon chromatic degrees of the scale have been used very little, though more since the thirties. Examples are to be found on the sharpened tonic (or flattened supertonic), sharpened subdominant, flattened submediant, and flattened leading-note.

The seventh on the flattened supertonic (known as the 'augmented sixth') is a chord much used in modern jazz variations as a substitute for dominant harmony. It is not found much in sheet music, but there are examples in 'Stompin' at the Savoy', 'All God's children got rhythm', and 'East St. Louis Toodle-oo'.

'East St. Louis Toodle-oo' (bars 26–28). Published 1927

Dm   A⁷   Dm   A⁻⁹ E♭⁷   Dm

×*Seventh on flattened Supertonic*

and known as the "German Sixth"

Composers of the fifties used sevenths other than normal sevenths built on the chromatic degrees of the scale for the sake of greater harmonic freedom, for variety, modulation, or during sequential passages.

During the twenties diminished chords were used a good deal, particularly those on the sharpened tonic (or flattened supertonic), sharpened supertonic (or flattened mediant), and sharpened sub-dominant (or flattened dominant); the diminished seventh was usually added too.

'Cornet Chop Suey': Introduction. Published 1924

E⁶ G♭o⁶ B♭⁷

×*Diminished seventh chord on flattened third*

'Cornet Chop Suey': Section B (bars 28–30)

× *Diminished seventh chord on sharpened fourth*

Diminished chords hardly appear in sheet music of the thirties. In the modern era (since 1940) those which have been used are usually built on diatonic bass notes.

CHROMATICALLY ALTERED CHORDS

Lastly, there are the 'chromatically altered' chords which are useful for colouring or modulation. There are three kinds:

(i) The normally major chord may be replaced by its minor form:

'Cornet Chop Suey': Section B (bars 25–28)

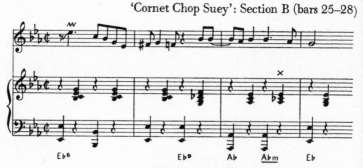

×*Subdominant Major chord replaced by Minor form*

The major seventh is sometimes added for further decoration.

(ii) The expected minor chord may be replaced by its major form, and the seventh added.

'All the things you are' (bars 5–8)

×*Modulation to Cmaj.*

(The logical, nearly-related key is C minor with E flat as the melody note.)

(iii) A major chord may be replaced by an augmented one. Augmented chords have never been used much in sheet music, although the dominant chord with augmented fifth appears from time to time during the thirties.

'Body and Soul' (bars 1–2). Published 1930

×*Dominant chord with augmented fifth*

Copyright 1930 by Chappell & Co. Ltd. Renewed and assigned to Harms Inc. Used by permission.

The modern era sometimes uses the tonic chord with augmented fifth.

PEDAL NOTES

Pedal notes are sometimes used in the harmonization of popular music; they offset the chromatic movement of the chords. In Gershwin's 'There's a boat that's leaving soon for New York', there is a nine-bar 'double' dominant pedal note at the end of the middle section; the dominant is held in the vocal line as well as the bass, while the harmony moves in chromatic sevenths. A shorter dominant pedal of four bars' duration appears at the end of 'All the things you are'. An eight-bar pedal-point occurs in the John Lewis composition, 'Django'*, effecting modulation to B flat minor:

'Django' (bars 27–35) Key F minor. Published 1955

CONCLUSION

Judging from analysis of chords used in the tunes listed on pp. 81–82 it seems that the increased use of chromaticism is much tied up with the more extended use of sevenths; since the forties more 'normal' sevenths are built on chromatic degrees of the scale and there has been a sudden enormous rise in the use of other seventh chords which involve chromatic notes.

In this context it is interesting to observe that the modern era seems to favour chords with a minor foundation in much the same way as the twenties seemed to prefer major ones; perhaps this inclination towards the minor contributes to the 'cool' effect of modern jazz.

It must be remembered that the jazzman is a practical musician. He *hears* these combinations of sounds; he does not learn them from a textbook. The chord-symbol system itself summarizes the aural effect of harmonies; it does not reflect any theory about them. It must also be borne in mind that a comprehension of the chord-system does not make a jazz musician; what counts is the way in which the improviser applies his knowledge and feeling.

2. Forms

The form of a normal jazz item is that of theme and variations. This is an age-old musical form which has nevertheless remained popular as a challenge to musicians right up to the present day: jazz—improvised or written—is one of its latest manifestations. A tune in simple two- or three-part form is played and then repeated many times, each time with a variation which gives the original theme new interest.

This form is used because of all forms it is the best suited to improvisation. Spontaneous on-the-spot composition and instant performance, without the tedium of writing to impede the flow of thought, has obvious attractions for a fertile musical mind. Many great composers were during their lifetime equally famous as improvisers, their concern with music as an improvisatory form being as important to them as the transferring of their thoughts to paper. How interesting it would be if we had recordings of these men's improvisations! Who knows what treasures of melody, harmony, and rhythm have been lost for all time because of the absence of any means of recording? Only recently have composition and improvisation been thought of as two separate arts. During the eighteenth century every performer was expected to improvise his own cadenza. Earlier performers were expected to improvise over a figured bass, and in the seventeenth century, in the early days of instrumental music, to improvise variations on a given melody. Jazz, as one of the twentieth century forms of improvisation, represents an ancient and important element in music.

Clearly, the player has to be conversant with the harmonic progression of a number before he can improvise, since all his variations are based upon the harmony and fit over it. To all intents and purposes, a jazz musician is improvising on a figured bass, for his chord sequence is established; but in contrast to a figured bass which is read from a score, the jazzman has to memorize the chord sequence. Inasmuch as his sequence of chords is repeated for each chorus, he is virtually performing an extended chaconne.

A musician indulging in variation form is judged by his inventiveness in applying the three-fold possibilities of melodic, rhythmic, and harmonic variation. Jazz uses, for the most part, the melodic type. Rhythmic variation is usually implicit, although sometimes there may be a complete change of tempo or even of time signature, 4/4 or 2/4 to 3/4 or vice versa, melody and harmony often remaining unchanged. (In jazz the 2/4 or 4/4 time signature has always been popular, the 3/4 or 5/4 since the middle fifties.)

The harmonization of the theme is established at the very beginning of the performance and then maintained. This harmonization may be the original, or it may be new; chords may be completely changed or else elaborated, either by the inflection of notes within the chord or by the addition of other notes. Another form of harmonic variation is to play in a different mode from the original— major to minor or vice versa.

There are four main methods of melodic variation:

(I) *Theme paraphrase.* The general outline of the theme is maintained so that, although there are changes of detail, the listener is able to 'follow the tune' and recognize it easily. The 'announcement' of the theme in jazz performance is often a mild paraphrasing of the melody and harmony as set out in the sheet music edition.

(II) *New melody replaces some parts of the paraphrase* (a mixture of I and III). Although the soloist mixes the paraphrasing of the theme with certain departures from it, the listener still has plenty to 'hold on to' in the way of familiar material, and can follow the theme at least in outline. The relationship of variation to theme is pretty obvious to the ear.

(III) *Complete new melody replaces the theme.* The adventure really begins here for listener as well as soloist. The improvised solo takes flight from its familiar territory; the only common factor between it and the theme is the harmony. Herein lies the whole art of the jazz musician.

(IV) *The theme may be used canonically or fugally.* This

method of variation has been used notably by certain present-day jazz musicians.

To discuss these in more detail:

(I) *Theme paraphrase.*

This may be effected by:

1. Rhythmic changes: even notes may be 'dotted' (or vice versa); notes may be repeated where they were previously held (or vice versa).
2. Melodic omissions: notes may be omitted, thus 'simplifying' the theme: the soloist may remain silent (tacet) at the phrase-opening, then enter later.
3. Melodic additions by the use of customary devices, such as passing notes (unaccented and accented), arpeggio notes, auxiliary notes mordents, turns (especially useful for the first note of a phrase), or tonal effects (see later section of this chapter).
4. Note changes: occasional notes may be changed enharmonically, or replaced by others which fit with the harmony.

There is a recording of 'Panama'* made by Kid Ory's Creole Jazz Band (trumpet, trombone, clarinet, piano, guitar, string bass, drums) which illustrates a number of these points. Here is an outline of the form:

Key: Section A: F.   Sections B and C: B flat.
Form:

 Introduction: 4 bars

 Section A (16 bars) 2 choruses ⎫ Ensemble
 Section B (16 bars) 2 choruses ⎬ Theme-paraphrase
 Section C (16 bars) Variation 1 ⎭ on trumpet

     Variations 2–4 Clarinet
     Variations 5–6 Collective improvisation

Notice that the piece ends in a different key from the opening. If you compare the recording with the sheet music you will see that only the first sixteen bars of A are used and then repeated: the longish coda in the sheet music is omitted from the recording.

The opening Section A is as follows. (The lower stave shows the original melody according to the sheet music edition, the upper stave the trumpet paraphrase.)

Transcribed AD

ANALYSIS

Phrase 1 (bars 1–4) paraphrase of melody. Original melody pretty well intact, but:

Tiny rhythmical changes in bars 1, 3, 4.

Bar 1. Unaccented passing note added: D sharp.

Bars 2. D enharmonically changed to D sharp.

Bar 4. One note changed from D to F, but it fits with the harmony.

Phrase 2 (bars 5–8) breaks away from the original melody more than the first phrase; the trumpet solo is more simple than the original melody.

Bar 5. A new melody which fits over the harmony.

Bar 6. Identical to original melody, but one note is omitted.

Bar 7. Economical—tacet for two beats, then F for a half-bar, making a discord.

Bar 8. Identical to original, but for a tiny rhythmic change.

Phrase 3 (bars 9–12). As in Phrase 1, the original melody is pretty well intact, but:

Tiny rhythmical changes in bars 9, 11, and 12.

Bar 9. A second F added on the fourth beat.

Bar 10. E substituted for D

Bar 11. C and A replace the four quavers of the original melody.

Bar 12. An auxiliary G is added on the second beat.

Phrase 4 (bars 13–16). Only six notes are identical with the theme (marked with crosses) while the rest is quite different. Incidentally, the harmony is changed from the original at bars 13 and 14.

Despite these differences, there is sufficient of the original melody retained in fact or in spirit for the listener to keep his ear on the tune and to recognize it as the theme of 'Panama'. The original melody, according to the sheet music, is never stated, even at the outset. It is assumed that the listener already knows it.

The second part (Section B) of 'Panama' offers a different kind of theme-paraphrase, again by the trumpet.

Transcribed AD

[1]

Original melody

[5]

[9]

[13]

ANALYSIS

A very 'economical' variation for the most part; many notes of
the original melody are omitted, the bare outline of the tune being
retained—a kind of 'précis' of the original. Conversely, notice the
following *additions* to the theme:

Unaccented Passing Notes decorating the anacrusis before bar 1.

Bar 7. Upper auxiliary note D.

Bar 11. Lower auxiliary note C sharp.

Bar 16. One-bar 'break' filling in the bar.

(II) *New melody replaces some part of the theme-paraphrase*
The first chorus Section C (trumpet) shows a break-away from
the theme-paraphrase from bar 10 onwards.

Transcribed AD

ANALYSIS

Bars 1–8 are a paraphrase of the melody.

Bar 10. Notice the silence preceding bars 11–15: these constitute
a new melody well away from the theme, but based on the same
harmonies. Basically, bars 13–15 are:

(III) *Complete new melody replaces the theme*

The old proverb 'One good turn deserves another' may well be adapted to 'One good *tune* deserves another'. A variation which 'replaces' the theme stands or falls according to its success as a good melody in its own right. A jazz soloist succeeds or fails according to his ability to invent an attractive 'new melody' (variation) to fit over the harmony. Much use is made of arpeggio passages and scale passages which are virtually 'arpeggio-based' passages decorated by passing notes, appoggiaturas, neighbouring notes, suspensions, changing notes, notes of anticipation, and blues notes. (More of these last later in the chapter.)

Let us take a look at some of these devices in action; here is 'Panama' Section C Third Chorus, for clarinet.

Transcribed AD

ANALYSIS

Even from a cursory glance at this clarinet solo it is immediately clear that all paraphrasing of the original melody has been thrown to the winds. The solo is an entirely new melody built over the harmony of the theme. Notice the following:

(1) Balance of stepwise and leaping passages.

(2) Arpeggios in bars 8–9 and 11–12.

(3) Decoration of the essential chord notes:

Bar 1. Accented passing note E flat.

Bar 2. Appoggiatura C sharp.

Bar 4. Unaccented passing notes. B flat and G.

Bars 6 and 9. Auxiliary note A.

(4) The long sustained G in bars 13–15. First it makes an added sixth over tonic harmony, then an added ninth over dominant seventh harmony; finally it forms a suspension over the tonic chord. Notice further how the resolution is decorated by the use of changing notes (marked with a cross).

A jazz musician not only has to invent new melodies. When he works in a group which is 'ad-libbing'—that is, making up the music as it goes along—he also has to invent *counter*-melodies, which not only fit the harmony, but complement the other parts too. This happens in 'Panama', First Chorus, Section C (quoted above, p. 22) where the trombone and clarinet back the trumpet theme-paraphrase. These are the trumpet and trombone parts:

Transcribed AD

In this performance of 'Panama' there are no less than six repeats of Section C and the fifth one is a good example of *collective improvisation*. In this chorus each of the three melody instruments *at the same time* improvises a melody which fits the harmony, thus making three-part counterpoint. Apart from one moment in the trumpet part in bars 8 and 9, there is no resemblance to the original melody of 'Panama'.

Transcribed AD

Observe the notes of anticipation in the clarinet part, bar 5 (marked with a cross).

NEW DEVELOPMENTS

There has been a growing feeling since the forties that jazz needs to stretch its horizons to something more than improvisation upon diatonic and chromatic chord progressions. Moves have been made (as in non-jazz music at the turn of the century) to base jazz upon the modes: jazzmen have experimented with atonalism and improvisation of note rows (see later), and obviously they can try out all the other resources of the non-jazz world which so far have not been attempted—for example, microtonality and polytonality. They may also be able to discover new improvisatory means of their own.

3. Scales

The tonality of most jazz is major, although there are examples in the minor mode, so it follows that its music is based on the major and minor scale system. However, much jazz melody—and the actual themes used for variation—is influenced by the vocal style of the Blues, the largely improvised folk-song of the Negro people. Not only is jazz instrumental tonal quality imitative of the vocal style, but its actual melodic shape and inflexions reflects the blues, work songs, and spirituals of the Afro-American Negro.

Although many of these songs are in the major mode, Negro melody has a strong link with the pentatonic scale, a simple five-note scale which is ubiquitous in folk music throughout the world, including Africa. The pentatonic scale avoids semitones:

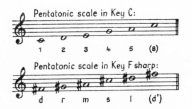

(The pentatonic scale in the key of F sharp uses only the black keys on the piano keyboard and is therefore easily memorized by piano beginners.) It is virtually the European major scale minus its fourth and seventh degrees.

Some old Scottish tunes—for example, 'Auld Lang Syne'—are built on the pentatonic scale. So is much Central European and Oriental folk music; so are many of the best-known Negro spirituals —'Swing low, sweet chariot', 'Deep River', 'Nobody knows the trouble I've seen':

The listener, without even realizing, is given a 'feeling' by this pentatonic effect; the peculiar message of the song is conveyed without words.

'BLUE' NOTES

As mentioned previously, the coloured slaves were surrounded by white man's music of European origin—particularly English, French, and Spanish—and it may well be that, hearing melodies built on the major scale, they tried to incorporate the fourth and seventh degrees into their own pentatonic melodic improvisations; but they subtly avoided the semitone intervals by slightly flattening the lower note. These slightly-flattened third and seventh degrees are so characteristic of the blues and blues-type melody that they are known as 'blue notes', and the resulting set of sounds the 'blues scale'. Sometimes the true major third and seventh are sung, but usually the singer takes the blue notes, seeming to attack the diatonic notes 'slightly flat', giving an almost 'out-of-tune' effect.

It is difficult to transcribe a blues since both melody and rhythm are bent and stretched very freely by the singer to suit the words and their mood. Here is a melody which illustrates the two blue notes:

Let us look at the blues scale in two contexts. If we consider the major and natural minor scales:

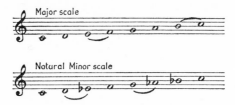

we find that the blues scale is a major scale which tends towards minor tonality on its third and seventh degrees; in a way, it is bi-modal! If we consider the Dorian mode—a scale consisting of the equivalent of all the white keys from D to D on the piano keyboard:

we find that the blues scale approximated very closely, except that in the Dorian mode the third and seventh degrees are fixed a semi-tone above the second and fourth degrees; but in the blues scale, these degrees *may* appear as in the major scale, or *slightly flattened* as blue notes.

It is obvious that blue notes give a 'twist' to the modality of a melody—a feeling of hovering twixt major and minor. This phrase

is obviously in C major, but the blue note on the third degree gives
an effect of being momentarily in C minor:

In written jazz, blues notes are indicated as flattened notes, but
the jazz player interprets them accurately—that is, as only *slightly*
flattened. To achieve the effect of a blue note on the piano, the
pianist sounds the diatonic and flattened note *together* in the same
chord, either in one hand as a minor second, or divided between the
two hands:

this again gives the effect of uncertain tonality, because the vibra-
tions conflict and cause a vibrato within the two sounds. Blue notes
affect the diatonic harmony; two typical endings illustrate this.

In (a), the diatonic major key established with the two appearances
of C major chord is disputed by the two blue notes, sounded over
dominant harmony, making it into the dominant thirteenth, with
the thirteenth slightly flattened!

(b) Instead of finishing on the tonic chord, the added blue note gives the inconclusive effect of ending on a chord of the seventh.

Many popular tunes have adopted the melodic-harmonic devices of the blues. A number of them do not end with the semitone rise from leading note to tonic, but more often approach the tonic by leap of a third from above or below:

F   C

G   C

a device typical of blues cadences. This is particularly evident at the end of slow numbers:

'Stormy Weather'

'Lover come back to me'

By permission of Lawrence Wright Music Co. Ltd., London W.1.
Copyright 1928 by Harms Inc. Used by permission.

In 'Stormy Weather', also notice the blue note (written as A sharp instead of B flat).

4. Rhythm

The rhythmic aspect of jazz is its most unique quality. The 'pulse' beat is always present—either obvious or implied—and over this are built various syncopated patterns.

The pulse is the even, regular throb which underlines all music; it is the life-giving heartbeat; in fact, it is most often referred to as 'the beat'. Tempo—that is, speed—is a matter of distance between pulses. For the most part, it is true to say that if pulses are close together, the music is fast, and if they are well apart the music is slow. Sometimes in slow jazz numbers—especially in blues and modern jazz—the underlying pulses are wide apart, but the improvisations are fast moving, so that the listener receives an impression of fast pulse, an effect known as 'double time'. The Miles Davis trumpet solo in 'All the things you are' (see p. 69) illustrates this, the underlying two-minims-in-a-bar pulsation being overlaid by a melody moving at the rate of four-crotchets-in-a-bar.

Conversely, an exciting effect is obtained when a slow-pulse melody is backed by a fast-moving accompaniment, created by dividing the pulse. This happens in the Beguine:

'When they begin the Beguine'

Although the basic metronomic-like pulse exists as the basis of jazz, there are times when over this the soloist allows his melodic line to vary in pulsation—going a little slower at one moment, then making up for lost time by going a little faster immediately afterwards—but ending at precisely the same moment as he would have done by keeping in strict time. This 'rubato' is used particularly in slow blues-like improvisations. In the Miles Davis solo referred to above, bars 3 and 4 are played 'rubato'—not strictly as the transcription implies. This device has obvious limitations in collective improvisation!

Another aspect of slight deviation from the exact pulse is the infinitesimal lengthening of certain notes, which underlines them without giving them any extra stress. Notes at the opening of a phrase are often sustained in this way, and likewise the extreme note of a rising passage (for example, the first note of bar I in the example above) or falling passage, or the penultimate note of a phrase. Underlining of this kind is implicit in the onward flow of the music and is known as an agogic accent (it happens while the music is 'agog'!) as opposed to the more obvious dynamic accent of force, indicated by the familiar sign > .

There are some moments in jazz when players are instructed to play 'colla voce'; then the pulse is temporarily allayed, the soloist moves freely in recitative style with no fixed rhythm, and the other musicians follow.

RHYTHMIC PATTERNS: SYNCOPATION

New Orleans jazz has two beats in a bar, but from the thirties onwards it is more customary to have four in a bar. (There was a popular song of the thirties called 'Bounce me brother with a solid four'.) But jazz may be in three-time, or even five-time, so long as it expresses the essential spirit of jazz.

Some dances are characterized by a 'germ' or 'snap' of time pattern, which is established and then more or less repeated over and over again as a rhythmic basis for the music.

Mazurka	(Polish)	**Moderato**
Bolero	(Spanish)	
Habañera	(Cuban)	**Slow**
Tango	(Afro-Spanish)	
Samba	(Brazilian)	
Conga	(Afro-American)	
Rumba	(Afro-Spanish)	
Charleston	(Afro-American)	
Beguine	(West Indian)	

The last five of these dances involve us in unusual accents. Although they are not jazz, they serve to illustrate the kind of syncopation which is a great feature of jazz rhythm, and they are also relevant, since jazz of the fifties and later experiments with the blending of Latin-American music and jazz. Syncopation is not new; but jazz is unusual in that syncopation is an essential feature of its rhythmic style.

If there are two (or more) players, syncopation may take place in one part whilst the other maintains normal pulsation. Alternatively, syncopation may be performed over an 'implied' pulse retained in the mind of performer and listener during the deviation from it.

(1) In 'special emphasis' syncopation stress is given to notes that would normally be unaccented.

(a) At the discretion of the player, accents are placed on notes normally unaccented (see examples on pp. 70 and 71).

(b) Rests occur at the normal point of accent, giving an interruption in the expected continuity of sound and a throwing of accent on to the following note (see example on p. 62).

(c) The normal grouping of sounds is altered by abnormal accenting. In 4/4 time the crotchet beats naturally fall into groups of two and four, giving duple and quadruple grouping. When the normal accent is shifted to beats 2 and 4, the result is 'off-beat' crotchets. But if the beats are grouped in threes, fives, or sevens, the result is uneven grouping of sounds within each bar.

The quavers of 4/4 time naturally fall into groups of four, but if we change the grouping to an odd number, three, five, or seven, the result is again uneven grouping of sounds within each bar. For example, triple grouping:

Notice how the accent changes from odd- to even-numbered quavers (and vice versa) within a bar. Over the three bars, each of the eight quavers in turn carries the accent, but only twice do 'normal' accents occur: at (a) and (b). Bar I is the familiar Rumba rhythm (see earlier in the chapter). The ultimate effect is of uneven grouping:

This gives a feeling that the bar is made up of three smaller bars of unequal length. A similar throwing of accent upon the fourth quaver of the bar occurs in the Charleston, likewise in the Conga in every other bar. In each of these dances there is a triple grouping of the first six quavers in the bar.

In the Samba the accent is placed on the second quaver of the bar.

These syncopations of triple grouping have been used ad infinitum by jazz musicians, largely at the expense of other possibilities.

For example, it is possible to syncopate with a quintuplet grouping over a series of five bars:

Perhaps it was the Spanish influence of the environment of jazz in its early days which caused the Rumba's triple grouping to be so favoured. It made an immediate appearance in ragtime piano music, where the right hand plays melodic patterns of three repeated notes in this rhythm:

(2) In 'anticipatory' syncopation a normal beat is anticipated by throwing the accent on to a usually weak beat (or part of a beat) which is then tied over, or sometimes followed by a rest. This kind of syncopation features greatly in spirituals, modern dance-music, and popular tunes as well as jazz.

In 'Deep River' bars 2 and 4 show syncopation on the second note, which is anticipated by one beat:

This could so easily have been placed squarely on the naturally accented third beat, instead of the second:

or a jazz example, see the example on p. 23, bar 13.

In 'Nobody Knows' the melody-note on the second beat of bars 1, , and 4 is anticipated by one quaver:

Without the quaver anticipation, this would sound as:

This is a very familiar, much-used device in popular music; for example:

'I want to be happy'

For jazz examples, see pp. 19 and 22.

A spiritual which combines the use of anticipatory crotchets and quavers is 'Swing low, sweet chariot':

Compare it with syncopation:

The jazz musician also uses a more subtle form of anticipation hardly detectable by the listener as more than a 'feeling'. This is anticipation of a note by a semiquaver only. Thus the opening of 'All the things you are':

would be played as:

The anticipation of notes by a fraction of the beat is an important part of the vitality of jazz.

The 'swing' of jazz is baffling to analyse and describe; it is something which has to be caught rather than taught, and that is why a non-jazz musician finds the style so elusive. The underlying pulse must be metronomic, but there must also be minute variations of rhythm or dynamics which make the 'feeling'. The difference between a jazz brass section and a symphonic brass section playing an identical piece of dance music is apparent in the fact that one is 'feeling' it and the other is playing what is written.

STYLE

This brings us to the matter of exact note values. When a jazz musician is given a passage of quavers such as the following to play:

'You turned the tables on me'

He automatically interprets them as:

—or nearly so; for in fact, the resulting rhythm is nearer to a triplet than a quarter division of the beat:

It is a style peculiar to jazz musicians, known as delayed syncopation.

All this involves obvious complications in writing; although Example C is the nearest to exact rhythm, it is more convenient to write as in Example B for written orchestral arrangements of jazz and dance music when non-jazz musicians (especially string-players) are often required to perform. When Leonard Bernstein composed the music for *West Side Story*, being well aware that his orchestra would include non-jazz as well as jazz musicians, he took great care in writing the orchestral parts, working on the lines of Example C in such a way that they would give a result as near to the jazz idiom as possible.

5. Tonal Effects

All the effects and devices discussed in this section are used in jazz to achieve the vocal quality, in an attempt to imitate the inflexions of the human voice.

Vibrato is a slight undulation of pitch. The effect is obtained by slightly sharpening or flattening a note alternately an equal distance above and below its true pitch. In jazz, vibratos of a great variety are used—wide and narrow, slow and fast, jerkily and gently undulating according to the mood of the music and the desire of the player or the composer. A player is often characterized by his vibrato style.

Reed players use lip vibrato, produced by opening and shutting the jaws; trumpeters use the fingers on the valves to shake the instrument; and trombonists either employ lip vibrato or sometimes move the slide up and down.

Players of traditional jazz often play with a rapid vibrato in imitation of the Negro singing voice. Modern jazz players generally either use a much slower vibrato or none at all.

Glissando—lit. 'sliding' from one sound to another, passing microtonally through many sounds upwards or downwards. This effect is used not only in jazz—for example it is used in Khachaturian's 'Sabre Dance'. In jazz, the glissando really came into its own in the idiom of the New Orleans trombone style, and it has been used ever since; the effect is also used by other instruments; for example, the famous ascending clarinet glissando—of about an octave and a half—at the opening of Gershwin's *Rhapsody in Blue*. Long notes may be decorated by making a glissando to the next note.

The Smear is virtually a very short microtonal glissando. The performer approaches a note from slightly below its exact pitch, holds the out-of-tune effect for the desired length of time, sometimes for most of its value, sometimes less, then slides up to the real note just at the end, satisfying the listener that the real note was intended. Similar effects are used in Oriental music. The smear is a typical jazz sound, similar to the change of pitch of blues notes: it is mostly used in slow blues and ballads or blues-type numbers, it is especially useful for decorating the first note of a phrase.

The Fall is a reverse of the smear. The performer plays the exact note and then falls off it rapidly, as much as a third to an octave in a very short space of time, with an indeterminate ending.

The Bend is a slow microtonal mordent, which may take the upper or lower auxiliary note. Long notes may be decorated by 'bending'.

Growl—a 'growling' effect is achieved by singing into the instrument a note other than that being played. This can be enhanced in brass instruments by use of the plunger mute. A growl may also be produced by growling at the back of the throat and playing a note. Mostly used by brass players, the effect has also been used by saxophonists and clarinettists.

Flutter—short for 'flutter-tongueing'—is a fluttering effect produced on wind instruments by rolling an 'r' whilst playing. Originally attributed to Strauss, flutter-tongueing was first performed on the flute, but it is now considered to be quite successful on most wind instruments.

Mutes and their effect. Brass instruments have a bright sound, but they may be muted to make them quieter or to alter the tone-quality. Muted instruments may be used for solo or team work. There are two types of mute: those which are placed *near* or *over* the bell, and those which fit *into* the bell.

(1) *Those which are placed near or over the bell*

a) *Plunger;* (b) *Metal Derby*

These two mutes are both *plunger-type mutes*, being plunger- or bowl-shaped. A real plumber's plunger was used in the early days of jazz, and still is in many cases; alternatively, a small bucket, a glass, or a hat (bowler, U.S. 'Derby'). Nowadays, manufactured fibre plungers are often used and metal Derby hats. These are held over the bell to confine the sound in varying degrees by pressing the mute near to the bell in 'close' position, or tilting it to one side in 'open' position. The sound goes into the plunger and out at the sides; the closer the mute is pushed towards the bell, the more muffled the sound: when the plunger actually touches the bell, it buzzes. Sometimes the mute is moved continuously from close to open position in a fanning movement, alternately confining and releasing the sound, giving a closed and open effect known as the 'oo-ah' or 'ah-oo' sound. This effect was much exploited by the swing bands of the thirties, notably by Duke Ellington. Some trombone players add a small, straight mute in addition to the plunger; this keeps the notes more in tune.

(c) *The Bucket (or Tub) Mute*

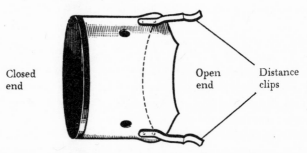

Closed
end

Open
end

Distance
clips

This is tub-shaped and made of fibre, lined with felt. The circumference of the mute and the bell of the instrument is identical. The mute is clipped into position, holding it at a set distance away from the bell, usually about half-an-inch, thus giving a uniform sound from the whole section. The sound goes into the tub, hits the resonator at the bottom, then out again. Its effect is softer and fuller than open brass—round and mellow. It is a most popular modern effect for teamwork, but can be used for solos.

(d) *Felt*

Occasionally a felt is used, either hung from or held to the bell of the instrument; this takes the 'edge' from the tone, whilst preserving the 'open' sound. This is a very mellow effect for sweet 'open' solos. It may also be used to get a 'horn' effect. It is used for solo and team work.

(2) *Mutes which fit into the bell*

These are hollow 'shapes' made of fibre, papier maché, or aluminium. All are open at the narrow end which goes into the bell. Those with a hole right through the middle fit right inside the bell, held in place by a cork band; the others are fitted with cork pads to hold them away from the sides.

(a) *The Straight or Fibre Mute*

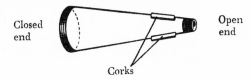

Closed end   Open end

Corks

This is cone-shaped with a flat end. It is made of fibre with a maple-wood resonator and has three corks which hold the mute away from the inside of the bell. The sound goes through the open end of the mute, hits the resonator, then comes back and out of the bell past the three corks. The straight mute gives a thin hard tone, often used for teamwork, but not so much for solos, although it is specially useful in Rumba and Samba trumpet solos.

(b) *The Cup or Hush Mute*

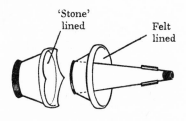

'Stone' lined   Felt lined

This is a straight mute with a cup added. The cup takes away the thin tone produced by the straight mute, because, as the sound escapes past the corks, it goes into the cup on the way out and becomes rounded. It gives a soft round tone which may be further softened by putting a cloth inside the cup. It is used for solo or team work; for the latter it is used closed, half- or three-quarters open; for solos, it is completely closed, giving a muffled, sweet, soft sound.

The Stone-lined Cup is used for team work. It has the cup sound, but more brittle and driving.

Both the straight and cup mutes are used in classical music. A famous example comes in the Strauss tone-poem *Till Eulenspiegel*, where muted trumpets and horns are used to describe Till being hanged on the gallows. Elgar used muted trombones with wonderful effect towards the end of the slow movement in his first Symphony.

(c) *The Harmon or Wa-Wa Mute*

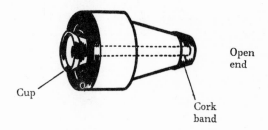

Open
end

Cup

Cork
band

This has two parts; the body is shaped rather like a spinning-top, and into this slides a tube with cup attached. It is made of aluminium and fits right inside the bell. The sound goes straight through the tube into the mute and out again. The player moves his hand over the cup to give the 'wa-wa' effect; otherwise the sound is light and 'crackly'. It is good for team work, most effective on trumpets; it is also used for solos, but not often for trombone.

Tin Mute. The harmon mute with cup removed is referred to as the tin mute by dance-musicians. It is used as a distance effect for solo or team work.

(d) *The Mega Mute*

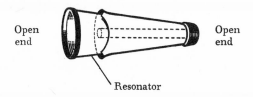

Resonator

This is cone-shaped with a tube through the middle; it is made of fibre with maple resonator, and fits right into the bell. The sound goes straight through, but the mute is so constructed that it does not thin out the tone; it gives a sweet, sonorous sound. It is much favoured for solo work, mostly for trombone; not much for trumpets.

Each mute can be used in various ways—fully closed, quarter- or half-open or almost open—to give different effects of volume or tone quality. With each mute, the player could thus have at least four different effects, if desired.

PART TWO

THE DEVELOPMENT OF JAZZ STYLES
AND INSTRUMENTATION

*(Asterisks beside jazz titles refer to the recorded performances
listed in Appendix B)*

The Pre-Jazz Era

The African elements contributory to jazz fall mainly into three
classes: Work Songs, Play Songs, and Religious Music.

WORK SONGS

The slaves who worked in the cottonfields and railroads of the
Southern States of North America were Negroes either imported
directly from Africa or descended from older slaves. Africans have
music and dance for every occasion, including work. Work songs
are 'functional' music—music to make work easier by arranging
for unanimous maximum effort at a particular moment in a song. A
number are based on the (solo) call-and-(group) response plan that
sea shanties often use; 'hollers' have a special cry as their response.
Many original African work songs were handed down aurally,
whilst new ones in the same tradition were extemporized on the job
and perpetuated.

In the Huddie Ledbetter (Leadbelly) recording of 'Take this
hammer'*, instead of the action taking place on a syllable the su-
preme effort is indicated by a united grunt, the blow of the hammer
falling at the end of each line.

Vigorously

Take this Ham-mer (Wow!) and carry it to the Cap-tain
(Wow!) Take this Ham-mer (Wow!) and carry it to the Cap-tain
(Wow!) Take this Ham-mer (Wow!) and carry it to the Cap-tain
(Wow!) You tell him I'm gone (Wow!) You tell him I'm gone (Wow!)

PLAY SONGS: THE BLUES

Melodically and rhythmically the work songs and blues have much in common. So far as historians can make out, the blues became widely popular during the latter part of the nineteenth century. They are a blending of folk poetry and song which usually falls into a strict pattern of three lines of poetry and twelve bars of music.

The words of the blues are simple rhyming couplets in iambic pentameters, the first line being repeated (either exactly or with slight variation) before the second is stated, thus making three lines in all. Each line of the poem takes four bars of music, hence the term 'twelve-bar blues'—but occasionally there are variants of this pattern, some containing eight and some sixteen bars. Usually each bar has four beats.

Not all blues are sad; there are happy ones too. Blues are, in fact, the folk-song of the negro, and, as in all folk-song, speak the hopes, fears, and experiences of a people—songs of 'play' inasmuch as they deal with all aspects of life except 'work'. These were the true Country Blues, which wandering minstrels perpetuated, carrying them all over the country, often, like Blind Lemon Jefferson, acompanying themselves on guitar. Sometimes the blues are sung in a recitativo style, with a half-speaking, half-singing voice known as 'blues-shouting'; a leading exponent is Joe Turner.

In contrast to the intimate, meditative folk-style of Country Blues, accompanied by guitar, the City Blues are extravert and more crisply rhythmic, designed to appeal to a larger audience, with a more glamorous accompaniment in the form of an instrumental group. The woman blues singers—so-called 'Classic Blues' performers—often used jazz musicians as accompanists.[1]

Blues melody is discussed on pages 27–31. The harmony originally fell into a regular twelve-bar pattern, as follows:

Where the lines of the poem do not use the full four bars of the music, the instrumental accompaniment fills in with an improvised 'break'.

The folk-style blues on page 29 has a harmonic formula very close to that quoted above:

While one of the Ma Rainey Classic Blues varies from it considerably, particularly in the second line:

---

[1] 'Rhythm and Blues' is a later development of the blues formula.

As time went on, these variants became numerous; indeed the blues as a basis for jazz is still a very live form. The title is sometimes given to pieces which retain the character of the blues, without keeping strictly to its harmonic formula.

RELIGIOUS MUSIC

The *Gospel Song* appears to be virtually a marriage between the emotional English non-conformist hymn and the work-song blues. Gospel songs are often improvised during service and may, like the work songs, fall into the call-and-response pattern. Many people consider that jazz is much more closely allied to the rhythmic hand-clapping and footstamping that accompany gospel songs and spirituals than to the African drum rhythms. A very joyful hymn is sometimes called a 'Jubilee'. The fervent participation in their 'syncopated hymns' is something very remote from the Western conception of reverent quietude as an expression of worship, but hymns without beat are to the Negro religion without God. It is as natural, and no more naïve, for them to sing hymns in this style as it was for Renaissance painters to portray Christ in Italian dress and environment.

Spirituals are Negro hymns—the Negro's own musical treatment of a message brought to him by his white enslavers. To him the Christian message was one of hope for something better to come, even if it must be in the afterlife. The slaves associated themselves with the Children of Israel being led to a better land and since many slaves worked on the railroads, the symbolism of a train on its way to heaven often occurs in spirituals; for example, 'Get on board, little children'. (The melodies and rhythms are dealt with in Part I.)

Some spirituals are in an extempore style—almost like a recitative—and others are of the 'regular beat' type. Singers often decorate the melody in jazz style with improvisation around certain notes and words.

MINSTREL SHOWS

During the early part of the nineteenth century, a white man journeying in the Southern States was so impressed by the style of music he heard the slaves singing, that he devised an entertainment in which performers made-up and dressed as 'minstrels' and sang music in similar style. These Minstrel Shows maintained their popularity throughout the century and were still in existence in the 1920s. The singing was accompanied by an instrumental group in which the banjo was prominent and drum rhythms an important feature. The shows included all the popular songs and dances of the day and were thus fertile soil for the latest in popular musical developments. Some people consider that minstrel music led to ragtime piano-playing.

Ragtime and Early Jazz

Towards the end of the nineteenth century ragtime music was becoming increasingly popular in America. Essentially piano music, it was partly inspired by the military march and cakewalk; this accounts for its strict two- or four-time and the way it falls into well-defined sections. The left hand plays simple harmonies largely based on the primary triads in 'downbeat', 'upbeat' style in imitation of the banjo vamp style; the downbeats (accents) are usually single bass notes, octaves, or tenths and the upbeats (weak beats) usually chords. The right hand is free to embellish the chord basis set by the left, with runs and arpeggios and much syncopation.

'Frog Legs Rag' (bars 1–8). James Scott

Cross-rhythms are accentuated by the shape of the melody; for example, figures of three notes within four-note groups.

Ragtime was popularized by being written down and circulated on sheet music and pianola rolls, but much was probably improvised, the style once having been set. Instrumental groups attempted to copy its style. The form of 'Frogs Legs Rag' (1906) is as follows :

Key :   Sections A and B : D flat.
                         Sections C and D : A flat.

Form :

Section I
Ternary
{
Section A twice—32 bars total.
Section B twice—32 bars total.
Section A once—16 bars only.
}

Link of 4 bars.

Section II
Binary
{
Section C twice—32 bars total.
Section D twice—32 bars total.
}

It is interesting to notice how the 'spirit' of the Rag is maintained throughout the two sections, although there is no material in common.

Traditional Jazz: New Orleans and Chicago

IMPROVISATION

The variations of the New Orleans and Chicago improvisers often stayed fairly close to the original melody, the variations being in the form of arpeggio and scale-like figures; passing and auxiliary notes and anticipations decorated the melody. The blues scale was always in evidence, as was the characteristic vocal quality of 'hot' vibrato tone with its growls and muted effects. The phrasing was in square two- or four-bar sections, with opportunities for 'breaks' (small cadenzas) at the end of each. These points are illustrated by the transcriptions from 'Panama' in Part I. During the twenties more and more importance was given to the solos and less to collective improvisation.

HARMONY

New Orleans and Chicago jazz was built upon blues, spirituals, stomps, marches, contemporary dance tunes, and original melodies. Most of the music was in the major mode, the diatonic triads and familiar progressions of simple European harmony forming the foundation of the numbers, with the additional colour of some chromatic harmony (see Part I: Chords). The most familiar progression of all was that of the traditional twelve-bar blues.

RHYTHM

Behind almost all jazz lies the reliable four-to-a-bar pulse beat. Until the changes of Bop in 1940, it was customary for the drummer to provide this steady beat on his bass drum with a pedal, embellishing this in various ways on the snare drum and cymbals. The rhythmic patterns created in the rhythmic and melodic improvisations on top of this basic beat often featured the dotted-quaver-semiquaver pattern in preference to two equal quavers, and there were many syncopated patterns which involved accenting of the second, fourth, sixth, and eighth quavers of the bar.

INSTRUMENTATION

Traditional New Orleans jazz was played in small groups, using 'front-line' of melodic instruments : one or two cornets or trumpets a trombone and a clarinet—plus a 'rhythmic-harmonic backing During the twenties saxophones began to be used more and more

The Fletcher Henderson Orchestra of 1923 used alto and tenor saxophones, and the Armstrong Hot Five recordings of 1926 find Johnny Dodds doubling on clarinet and alto saxophone. In a number of Chicago-style groups, the trombone was replaced by a tenor saxophone.

As time went on the rhythm group could be a collection of almost any of the following:

> tuba, sousaphone, string bass
> banjo, guitar, piano
> drums, washboard.

The drummer's kit consisted—and still consists—basically of bass drum with pedal-operated drumstick and a side drum with snares, played with drumsticks or wire brushes. To these are usually added two tom-toms, single cymbals and a pair of high-hat cymbals worked with a pedal. Additional effects are obtained from various woodblocks, cowbells, and so on (see p. 76).

FORM AND STYLE

In the melodic front-line, the cornet was the main voice around which the clarinet wove an obligato, and the trombone played something comparable to the tenor voice in four-part harmony. (See Part I: Variations.) The other instruments provided the backing the tuba (and, later, the string bass) supplied the rhythmic bass-line drums the strong, purely rhythmic background, while the banjo (the only non-military instrument) was an additional rhythmic armonic support. A similar role was played by the piano, but as it was not easily transportable for open-air functions, it was only used when jazz was played indoors for dancing. In section work, the pianist underlined the metrical beat in vamp style, the left hand playing single notes on the accents, doubling the bass line, the right hand playing chords, usually on all four beats, doubling the banjo part. The essential of New Orleans style was its collective improvisation of the front line with strong rhythmic background from the rhythm section; breaks and occasional solos gave a contrast of colour to the general effect. There is often a four-bar introduction to the polyphonic ensemble.

Here are two contrasting examples of the form used at this time. The first is 'Dippermouth Blues'*, recorded in 1923 by King Oliver's Creole Jazz Band (7 players)

Key: F
Form: Introduction: Nine choruses (12 bars each). Coda.
       Introduction: 4 bars.
       2 choruses: ensemble.
       2 choruses: clarinet.
       1 chorus: ensemble.
       3 choruses: cornet.
       1 chorus: ensemble.

Although this is a twelve-bar blues with a 'normal' blues harmonic progression, the phrasing of the melody is very unusual, riding across the square four-bar phrases set by the harmony. Notice the blues third at the end of bar 4.

Compare the phrasing of the clarinet solo in the third chorus. The recording is in key C; notice the variation of harmony in sever places.

Transcribed AL

The other example of form is 'Cornet Chop Suey',* recorded in 1926 by Louis Armstrong and his Hot Five (cornet, trombone, clarinet, piano, banjo).

Key: E flat
Form:

		Introduction:	4 bars.	
Theme	{	Section A:	16 bars.	} Trumpet solo
		Section B:	32 bars.	
Variations	{	Section B:	32 bars.	Piano Variation
			(only 4 bars on sheet music edition)	
		Bridge passage:	16 bars.	Cornet solo
		Section B:	32 bars.	Cornet Variations
		Coda:	8 bars.	

This solo is considered by some to be the greatest of all Armstrong originals. In the announcement of Section B it is interesting to notice that five of the eight phrases begin:

but the variation gets right away from this repetition. (The harmonised version appears on p. 12.) An interesting variation of the original melody occurs at bars 21–24 of Section B.

Notice the new tension caused by the change of harmony, especially at the end of the phrase where F sharp diminished harmony is superimposed on a dominant bass B flat.

Chicago saw the natural development of the New Orleans style, on the one hand by coloured musicians—such as King Oliver, Kid Ory, Louis Armstrong—on the other by white men—such as Bix Beiderbecke—who sought to copy it. With the development of technique, the soloist gradually became more important and the characteristic pattern was:

> Ensemble chorus.
> Solo chorus from each instrument.
> Ensemble chorus.

'Chicago-style' is usually the tag given to the white man's development of New Orleans style in the 1920s.

Skiffle is a simple form of jazz—in fact, traditional jazz in miniature—played upon a mixture of authentic and improvised instruments; the latter could include kazoo, comb-and-paper, jug, swanee whistle, cheesebox banjo, washboard. The essential remained, however, that the music was improvised, largely upon the blues and stomps. Skiffle is said to have originated in Chicago at the end of the twenties when there was not much money about, but the so-called *Spasm Bands* popular in the 1890s fulfilled the same sort of purpose, being composed almost entirely of improvised instruments.

The skiffle revival—a short-lived affair—began in England in 1954 with Lonnie Donegan and Ken Colyer. Performed in small groups, the essential was a front-line vocal melody (often blues and other folk-song) with a rhythm backing of guitar, bass, and washboard and possibly other percussion.

BOOGIE-WOOGIE

About the same time as Chicago was the focal point for jazz, certain pianists were popularizing boogie-woogie, a blues-based piano style which had probably existed since the turn of the century. The left hand plays in imitation of a strumming guitar, using a repeated bass pattern, often with eight notes in a bar:

giving the music great rhythmic drive. This rhythmic pattern is based upon the harmonies of the twelve-bar blues, and the right hand plays variations upon this sequence of chords. Two familiar forms of left hand are:

A good example of boogie-woogie is 'Honky Tonk Train Blues'*, recorded in 1927 by Meade Lux Lewis.

> Key: G major
> Form: Introduction   4 bars.
>   12-bar Blues: 8 times.
>   Coda: 2 bars.

Within these limits, Meade Lux Lewis builds a descriptive piece depicting a train 'gettin' started', 'pickin' up', 'goin' fast', and finally 'blowin' into the station'. A perfect example of boogie-woogie programme music!

The following left hand pattern is maintained *throughout the piece*:

It begins with a two-hand tremolo, typical of boogie-woogie introductions and interludes:

Later in the piece, the composer uses a right-hand tremolo over the rhythmic figure of the left hand:

Cross-rhythms are often used between the two hands:

Notice the clash of the left hand B natural with the right hand B flat. Chromaticisms of this kind add to the excitement and colour of the boogie-woogie style, giving the effect of the blues third.

The thirties: New York and the Swing Era

Typified by 'big' bands, this was the period of arranged jazz, later labelled as 'swing'—that is, music largely written down in imitation of jazz improvisatory style, some of it forming a background over which soloists could improvise. To some extent this style met the desire, for commercial reasons, to bring jazz more in line with the dance music of the time, and to make it more orthodox by European standards, where improvised music has largely become a forgotten art.

IMPROVISATION

Swing musicians used a less hot tone than their predecessors: their improvised melodies were more highly decorated versions of the original tune, both melodically and rhythmically, and many were much more concerned with the possibilities of variations built on the harmonic basis of the theme than melodic variation.

HARMONY

The harmonies of the thirties explored further the use of chromatic chords used in the previous decade, and to these were added the chords of the major seventh and dominant ninth, eleventh, and thirteenth, as resolved or unresolved sounds. The following is transcribed from a Fats Waller piano solo of 'Let's pretend that there's a moon'.[1]

[1] Unavailable. Originally recorded on 'Fats Waller Favourites, No. 2'. HMV DLP 1118.

Transcribed AD

Notice in bar 15 that the harmony has been changed from the original so that the melody note A sounds as the dominant eleventh.

RHYTHM

During the thirties, syncopation often involved accenting the first, fourth, and seventh (Rumba rhythm) or second, fifth, and eighth quavers in a bar.

INSTRUMENTATION

With the arrival of the swing era came bigger dance-halls and bigger bands; in addition to the idea of making jazz 'orthodox', written arrangements were necessary because the increased size of the group made collective improvisation difficult to achieve. The New Orleans front line of three solo instruments was increased to make sections of brass and woodwind instruments, comparable to the sections of a symphony orchestra. The brass section included trumpets and trombones (which could be subdivided into two sections); the reed section included clarinets and saxophones; while the rhythm section remained as before. Big bands of the twenties had used arrangements, but now the idea became widespread.

Notice that although the term 'big band' is used, the *size* does not by any means compare with that of a symphony orchestra, but rather with that of a small chamber orchestra. The number of instrumentalists in the brass and reed sections varied, but was usually between three and five saxophones and between five and eight brass. This number was occasionally augmented by the addition of strings during the later part of the Swing period. The piano and saxophone were now firmly established as essential instruments.

The band used by Fletcher Henderson for his arrangment of 'When Spring comes peeping through' recorded in 1926 had eleven players:

Brass	Reed	Rhythm
3 cornets	clarinet	piano
trombone	alto sax	banjo
	tenor sax	sousaphone
		drums

The band for Benny Goodman's 1935 recording of 'King Porter Stomp' had fourteen players:

Brass	Reed	Rhythm
3 trumpets	1 clarinet	piano
2 trombones	2 altos	guitar
	2 tenors	string bass
		drums

Even Duke Ellington's 1940 band which recorded 'Take the A train' had only fifteen players.

Brass	Reed	Rhythm
3 trumpets	clarinet	piano
3 trombones	2 altos	guitar
	1 tenor	string bass
	1 baritone	drums

STYLE

The swing arranger often used the three sections to contrast or imitate each other in turn, and characteristic of the style was the 'riff', a short repeated phrase which is passed from section to section with gathering impetus, making an exciting effect in itself, and at its best giving inspiration to the soloist. Obviously the success of any band is dependent, not only on its soloists, but upon the arranger who orchestrates the music.

One of the first to arrange jazz was Fletcher Henderson; in the 1926 recordings of his band there is a futuristic sound, anticipating the famous swing bands of Benny Goodman, for whom Fletcher Henderson later became arranger. The saxophone, in its alto and tenor sizes in particular, now became an indispensable part of the group. The musicians (known as 'sidemen') in the reed section did a good deal of 'doubling'—that is, playing of more than one instrument, in order to meet the demands of different scores; in the Fletcher Henderson orchestra, the two reed players played a dozen instruments between them! 'Concert' jazz arrangements were experimented with, including strings, xylophones, marimbas, tubular bells, and almost every possible instrument. The technique of many instruments was greatly increased by the demands of arrangers.

In piano solos, until the late thirties, the characteristic style was known as 'stride'. The left hand played in downbeat-upbeat style, 'striding' from bass note to chord; this left hand style was akin to ragtime, but performed with greater rhythmic emphasis. Meanwhile the right hand improvised with an expressiveness well away from the formal, composed rhythmic patterns of ragtime. Two great exponents were James P. Johnson and Fats Waller.

The importance of the swing era is that during the thirties jazz became popular, and therefore a commercial success for the only time so far; the band leaders and star players were the teenagers' idols. Some famous bands from the swing era: Jimmy Lunceford, Benny Goodman, the Dorsey brothers, Artie Shaw, Glenn Miller, Chick Webb, Cab Calloway, Duke Ellington, Count Basie.

Alongside the big band movement and sometimes within the big bands themselves a good deal of *small group* work went on in various styles; among these were The Benny Goodman Trio and Quartet; the Quintet of the Hot Club de France with three guitars, violin, and string bass (including the famous guitarist Django Reinhardt and Stephane Grappelly, one of the most famous of jazz violinists); and, anticipating the next phase of development in jazz, musicians like Charlie Christian (guitar) and Lester Young (tenor saxophone), great innovators who improvised in a more economical, lyrical style not at that time fashionable.

Opposed to the developments of swing were the Revivalists, who wanted to re-establish jazz of the New Orleans style, which they felt was fast being swamped out of existence. Ever since, the two streams—traditional and contemporary—have had lively support from their respective followers.

Outstanding among the band leaders of this period was Duke Ellington; he set out to *compose* music in the jazz idiom, working and experimenting with his instrumentalists and arrangers, until he formulated the distinctive Ellington sound. Many of his compositions are like miniature tone-poems, in which he makes effective use of muted and growl brass techniques.

The arrangements and compositions are the result of much experiment with various combinations of instruments and unusual harmonization all in jazz style. Much of his success must be due to the fact that, like Bach, he has been able to write specifically for the instrumentalists in his group, some of whom have been with him for many years, so that the music has a very personal touch and meaning.

FORM

During this period the 12-bar AAB blues was still used as a basis, but less widely than the 32-bar AABA popular song. Many songs of the period have become 'standards' among jazz musicians. Even when the composition is original a similar pattern can be seen. Here is the form of Duke Ellington's 'East St. Louis Toodle-oo'* recorded on 22 March 1927. There were ten players (two trumpets, trombone, clarinet, tenor saxophone, alto and baritone saxophones, piano (Ellington), banjo, string bass, drums).

Key: Introduction and Section A: D minor. Section B: F.
Form:

	Introduction	8 bars	
	Section A	32 bars (AABA) Muted trumpet solo (28 bars in piano solo edition)	
Exposition	Section B	18 bars trombone solo	4 bars theme paraphrase then variation
	Section A (shortened)	16 bars clarinet solo (first 8 bars and last 8 bars of A)	

Development	Section B	twice	
		(i) trumpets 18 bars	
		(ii) 2 clarinets for 8 bars Variations trumpets for 10 bars Theme	
	Coda	8 bars muted trumpet derived from Section A	

This is a famous composition of Duke Ellington's, once used as his signature tune.

Section A. The theme of Section A is built on an alternation of tonic and dominant harmony, and each time the theme appears, it is accompanied by the following countermelodies:

Transcribed AD

The above is first heard as the 8-bar introduction, then is immediately repeated twice beneath the theme at the opening of Section A.

Transcribed AD

Notice the dominant harmony with flattened ninth in bars 2, 4, and 6:

Section B. If the piano solo version of 'East St. Louis Toodle-oo' carries the original melody, then the trombone solo is a variation except for four bars (bars 3–6).

The second time, Section B is played in the 'development' section by two clarinets: compare this with the melody in the piano version!

Transcribed AD

The Forties: New Inspirations: Bebop

INTRODUCTION

Swing music continued into the forties with gradually waning success and many of its techniques were absorbed by the world of commercial dance music. But a number of musicians—especially the younger ones—were restless for change. They found the arranged swing music dull, they were sick of its harmonic clichés, its rhythmic monotony, and above all its improvisatory limitations.

There was a night-club in New York run by an ex-musician who gave carte-blanche to jazzmen to play as they pleased, so 'Minton's' became virtually the nursery of modern jazz, for many of the experiments which took place there were to affect the trend of jazz right up to the present day. The innovations affected the melody, harmony, and rhythm of jazz; on the whole they made more demands upon the technique of the player than previously and also required academic knowledge of harmony. Off to a difficult start with much opposition from musicians as well as public, it was 1948 before the new jazz received general acclamation.

IMPROVISATION

Pioneer jazzmen of the early forties aimed for a clean break with everything typical of swing. They based their improvisations almost entirely upon the harmonic foundation, often constructing new compositions upon the harmonies of already-familiar popular songs.

Melodic improvisation was chiefly affected by the increased use of passing notes. In any case, by adding the sixth, seventh, ninth, eleventh, or thirteenth to a chord with all inflections and enharmonic versions, *any* note becomes a part of the chord and thus available for improvisation :

3rd   5th   6th   7th   9th   11th   13th

The opening of the trumpet solo 'All the things you are'[1] (Miles Davis solo) shows chromatic notes used freely over sustained chords:

Transcribed AD

Notice, too, how the passing notes in bar 3 give the effect of new harmonies, especially as the two Fs and the C are accented passing notes.

Eb9   Eb13

[1] Unobtainable. Originally recorded on 'Charlie Parker Memorial Album' Vogue LAE 12002. Later 'takes' of the same chord sequence but with different thematic line are recorded under the title 'Bird of Paradise'*.

As in other modern music passing notes no longer 'passed', but could remain unresolved at the end of a phrase (but both examples can be analysed as harmonized ninths):

'Anthropology'

Even the 'new' fashionable flattened fifth (q.v.) used melodically was unpredictable; sometimes it was resolved as in bar 2 of 'Anthropology' (p. 71) (F resolved to E flat)—and at others escapes the expected resolution, as in bar 5 of the same example (B flat leaps to E natural). These leaps, in themselves, were part of the unpredictable character of bebop—as the new jazz was called—all seemingly calculated to puzzle the layman.

Not only were the melody, harmony, and rhythm of bebop bewildering, though; even the phrasing was not easy to follow. Gone were the square, even-length phrases; now they varied in length and even bridged or broke the natural phrasing of the song upon which they were built. This shows well in the extract from 'All the things you are' on p. 69.

HARMONY

The 'standards' used for improvisation during the forties were either old standards which particularly appealed, or contemporary tunes with chord sequences of a more chromatic nature than the typical sweet numbers of commercial dance music, e.g. 'All the things you are'. Alternatively musicians created their own themes. Improvisers of the forties and fifties used all the sevenths and ninths and augmented chords that had been used before, but frequently inflected the basic notes of the chords, or added notes which did not strictly belong. Surprising new sounds resulted from making a note fit any chord by suitable voicing.

SUBSTITUTE CHORDS

Instead of using the existing harmonic pattern of popular tunes, many of the original chords were replaced by new ones. Take the opening of 'I've got rhythm':

and compare it with the corresponding phrase in 'Anthropology'*, which is based on the same number, a new thematic line being superimposed.

Notice the harmonization of bars 1–3:

This idea of substituting a descending chromatic chain of seventh chords (possibly with ninth, eleventh, and thirteenth added) for the original harmony was also used in harmonizing the blues.

Also characteristic was the use of the chord of the augmented sixth as a substitute for dominant harmony, as shown in the final cadence of 'Anthropology'.[1]

Notice, however, that the fifth of the chord is flattened.

A favourite harmonic device was to vary chords by flattening the fifth:

'Anthropology'

In the original song, this chord was an unadorned dominant seventh on D.

The flattened fifth was also likely to appear in the final tonic chord of a number, as in 'Anthropology' (above), where seventh,

---

[1] The orchestration and piano solo may be obtained from Bosworth and Co. Ltd. 14–18 Heddon Street, Regent St., London, W.1.

ninth, and thirteenth are added. (Alternatively a seventh, ninth or eleventh could decorate the ordinary tonic chord, as at the end of the first chorus of 'Anthropology'.)

'Anthropology'

The Aladdin idea of 'new tunes for old' manifested itself in new melodies being composed over familiar, well-loved chord sequences. 'Anthropology' and many others were derived from 'I've got rhythm': another favourite for this particular exercise was 'How High the Moon'.

RHYTHM

In general, the dominance of the dotted quaver-semiquaver pattern (so typical of 'old' jazz) diminished, and rhythmic patterns were frequently based on note values much closer to even quavers, with the occasional occurrence of triplets; the weak part of every beat was usually accented. One way and another there was now much greater rhythmic variety.

A feature of solos was to end a phrase with two short notes on the accent. This perhaps suggested the word 'bebop' and gave the new style its name. See the second example on p. 72.

The experiments of the young innovators affected particularly the rhythm group—piano, guitar, bass, drums. Up until now their function had been solely to give a strong 'solid-four' rhythmic-harmonic foundation to the music, but the new music embraced the group as a whole, each instrument being equally responsible for supporting the soloist melodically and rhythmically.

The drummer, aiming at a more legato effect, played the pulse beat on cymbal with his right hand, giving a light sparkling background to the music, while the bass drum was now reserved for special effects to support the soloist; the left hand was thus free to invent a variety of exciting counter-rhythms. Sometimes, having established the pulse, both hands worked on the counter-rhythms, which only *implied* the foundation beat.

The pianist gave up playing the rhythmic 'stride' left hand, often leaving the bass line entirely to the string bass. Instead he concentrated on playing single-note melodies with the right hand, while the left hand played occasional chords to underline important harmonies, known as 'feed' chords or 'comping'. Thus the old, familiar, steady four-to-a-bar vamp backing was rejected in favour of greater variety of rhythm.

The bass now played in legitimate 'col arco' as well as the familiar pizzicato style; he played more contrapuntally than before, and with much more rhythmic agility.

The electric guitar, a new instrument, took its place in jazz and the guitarist, through being amplified, was able to contribute single-string solos. In fact all the 'rhythm' instruments took solo parts.

A further consideration of 'Anthropology' (p. 71) will show the characteristic accenting of the second half of certain beats. Another rhythmic feature favoured by the beboppers is that of double time (see page 32) as shown in Miles Davis's opening of 'All the things you are' (p. 69).

INSTRUMENTATION

During the forties, as the popularity of big swing bands waned, there was a return to small group jazz; the brass and reed sections were represented by trumpet and alto (or tenor) saxophone respectively (the clarinet virtually disappearing), supported by piano, guitar, string bass, and drums. The rhythm section now played a much more significant role in the texture of the music than before. The baritone saxophone and trombone were to be used more in jazz of the fifties.

These small groups experimented with combinations of all kinds of instruments, but later Bebop was adapted to big band style by Dizzy Gillespie, Woody Herman, and Gil Evans in his scores for the Claude Thornhill Orchestra.

FORM AND STYLE

Popular songs, blues, and original themes continued to be the basis of much improvisation, but the forties began to see a number of attempts to adopt non-jazz forms and devices.

Here to show a typical sample of form, is 'Stompin' at the Savoy'* recorded in 1941 by Charlie Christian (guitar) with piano, trumpet, drums, and bass.

Key: D
Form: 14 choruses and Coda of 4 bars.

Solos: Trumpet   Choruses 1 and 2
        Piano   ,,   3 and 4
        Guitar   ,,   5, 6 and 7
        Trumpet   ,,   8, 9 and 10
        Guitar   ,,   11, 12, and 13
        Trumpet   ,,   14

Coda : Trumpet : 2 bars
        Guitar :   2 bars

The first chorus given out by the trumpet is a fairly straightforward announcement of the theme—a 32-bar chorus AABA. Although Section A is basically tonic and dominant harmony, it takes a good deal of concentration to follow the chromatic solos which are woven above these two chords; the underlying chromatic harmony of the Middle 8 (Section B) makes a real 'release' and helps orientation. The cross-rhythms of the soloist are intricate but are set across a pretty solid four-to-a-bar from the drums, broken here and there to punctuate the solos. Important are the single-string solos on the electric guitar—an innovation in jazz; when not solo-ing, the old-style 'vamp' guitar can be heard behind the soloists.

Since the late 1940s, with the advent of the tape-recorder and long-playing record, the length of recordings is no longer bound by the limitations of the ten-inch 78 r.p.m. record.

The Fifties: Cool Jazz

In 1948, Miles Davis recorded with a small band which was to become a turning-point of modern jazz. It was a nine-piece group with written arrangements which married bop harmonies and rhythms to the Lester Young melodic style of improvisation. The result was cool jazz—cool, almost legitimate-toned music as opposed to the hot tone of traditional jazz and bebop, its variations economical, 'understated', and its relaxed rhythm giving the effect of being almost behind the beat. Cool jazz has mostly been the music of small groups, and instruments new to jazz have been introduced often effectively and successfully, including flugelhorn, French horn, flute, oboe, cello, and accordion. It was a period when jazz groups began using a wider variety of time signatures; musicians like Dave Brubeck added 5/4 and 11/4. In the previous decade Dizzy Gillespie had experimented with Latin-American and Afro-Cuban rhythms, and now many groups were embracing these ideas.

The instruments used in jazz of the fifties and still common today are as follows:

Brass: trumpet, trombone
Woodwind: clarinet, alto, tenor and baritone saxophones, flute
Rhythm: piano, guitar, double bass, drums, vibraphone
Occasionally, a group of strings is used.

The chief Latin-American instruments are

Fingerdrums: two small bongoes and a large conga
Cowbell hit with a stick
Tambourine
Rattles: chocolo (tube-shaped) and a pair of maracas (round, with handles)
Claves: two thick, hardwood sticks clapped together
Guiro: grooved bamboo scraped with a stick

During the 1950s there was a split amongst jazzmen in the U.S.A. Many New York musicians moved towards the West Coast, initially largely owing to the attractions which Hollywood offered. The film studios provided a good livelihood with the result that their jazz, now fashioned mainly for the recording studio, could afford to be experimental and even academic, now it was free from the necessity of being 'hard-sold' in the diminishing New York night-club scene. Their work was a logical continuation of the 'cool' movement, and most of the players were men with academic training behind them; as arrangers and composers this was obviously an essential requirement, and as players, the demands of reading and improvisation were extremely high.

Some of the orchestral compositions and arrangements by West Coast musicians lie so much in the border country between jazz and non-jazz that it is difficult to classify them as strictly belonging to either field: they are therefore called 'Thirdstream'.

The musicians were extremely versatile as instrumentalists, many of them doubling on several instruments (often a necessity in film-studio work), a number of them arranging and composing as well as playing. As many of them had studied composition, and the emphasis was upon *experiment*, they deliberately used non-jazz harmonies and forms in their music. Some critics considered the resulting jazz too cerebral, and that spontaneity was being pushed out.

Amongst the critics were the East Coast (New York) musicians. They felt that *emotional* expression was the important thing in all music and that unless technique and experiment can serve to further this, then the result is lacking in sincerity and conviction; Hard bop was an attempt to bring back the emotional content of bebop. East Coast composers and arrangers also experimented with classical devices and forms, especially counterpoint and fugue. A good comparison of the two styles—East and West—can be quickly made by listening to groups from the two schools.

During the 1950s much of the work in both East and West Coast schools was carried on in small groups of players with various combinations of instruments. Experiments were made with piano-less groups. The music, in all cases, was very largely arranged, but with opportunities for improvisation, the arrangements being either on specially composed themes or 'standards'.

BIG BANDS

The two important big bands which contributed most to jazz of the fifties were Woody Herman and Stan Kenton. Stan Kenton continued his 'progressive' experiments which often bordered on nonjazz territory; his music was closely linked with the West Coast since his sidemen were drawn from there.

MODERN JAZZ IN EUROPE

After the Second World War, and particularly during the fifties, the new-style jazz spread to the Continent through radio, recordings and tours of musicians. This was specially true of Sweden, France and England.

One of the first Continental countries to hear a live bebop performance was Sweden; there all things American have strong support and since Sweden was a neutral power, musical contacts were unbroken at the beginning of the war, at the time of the modern jazz innovations. Interest was thus stimulated in very early days.

French interest began in a rather different way. Certain American musicians went to live abroad after the war and a number were attracted to settle in Paris; there they inspired a 'school' of French modern jazzmen and created a live climate for jazz of all kinds.

However, musicians moved in both directions. While Americans were moving abroad, jazzmen from Europe were settling in the U.S.A. Other enthusiasts visited; from England came musicians working on the trans-Atlantic steamers, and these young men returned home fired with enthusiasm for what they had heard in New York.

Thus the jazz message was furthered. It has always been said that music is an international language and jazz is among the most international of all music. Such is its wide appeal that it is not surprising to hear jazz of all kinds in almost any country in the world.

The Sixties

So far, during this decade, the following for traditional and modern jazz has been maintained, but between the two extremes lies a class of music which is strictly in neither category, and this has come to be known as 'Mainstream'.

A hybrid is 'Thirdstream' music which is essentially composed, neither jazz nor non-jazz, but borrowing something from each. There have always been musicians who tried to blend the two traditions, but recently this has become a more feasible task, since modern jazz itself has already absorbed much of the European tradition, and academically trained composers with a foot in the two camps of jazz and non-jazz obviously find a challenge in the possibility of blending the two styles. William Russo and Gunther Schuller are leading Thirdstream composers.

Once more, young musicians are feeling an urge for change, a desire to break free from the limitations of improvising over a given chord sequence and a fixed time-signature; and so there is the 'New Wave' of modern jazz which concerns itself with experiments in modal, atonal, twelve-note, and serial possibilities as a basis for jazz. Here the innovators, as ever, improvise in a small group; they begin with an agreed theme, but after this the music is free to progress where it pleases, the players exchanging melodic, harmonic, and rhythmic ideas. Form and harmonies are not then tied to a progression, rhythms are not necessarily governed by a time-signature, and melodies are sometimes even unfettered by tonality.

The success of such music-making obviously depends upon the sympathy and alertness of the players within the group. It would seem that, in some ways, the discipline is greater than in other jazz, the player being almost less free than when working over a chord sequence. Some of the first to be active in this 'New Wave' were John Coltrane, Ornette Coleman, and Eric Dolphy—all three saxophonist composers—and Charles Mingus, bass player and composer.

Some consider that jazz improvisation will eventually be completely absorbed into composition, but this may well endanger the spontaneity which is the life-blood of jazz. Perhaps future jazz developments may run along two roads, one aiming at giving greater improvisatory freedom, and the other combining European-style composition with jazz techniques, each inspiring and vitalizing the other to maintain the unique identity which is jazz.

Appendix A: Some Tunes used as a Basis for Jazz ('Standards')

Title	Key	Composer	Publisher	Date
My gal Sal	B♭	Paul Dresser	Francis, Day & Hunter	1904
Frog Legs Rag	D♭ A♭	James Scott	Edwin H. Morris	1906
Panama	F B♭	William Tyers	Robbins	1911
After you've gone	B♭	Creamer and Layton	Francis, Day & Hunter	1918
Dippermouth Blues	E♭	Joe Oliver	Darewski	1923
When Spring comes peeping through	C	Bernard and Stept	Lawrence Wright	1924
Cornet Chop Suey	E♭	Louis Armstrong	Leeds	1924
Riverboat Shuffle	F	Hoagie Carmichael, Vownow, Mills, & Parish	Lawrence Wright	1925
East St. Louis Toodle-oo	Dm F	Duke Ellington & Bub Miley	Mills	1927
Body and Soul	C D♭ C	John Green	Chappell	1930

Title	Key	Composer	Publisher	Date
Let's pretend that there's a moon	G	Columbo, Hamilton & Stern	Chappell	1934
There's a boat that's leaving soon for New York	B♭	George Gershwin	Chappell	1935
Stompin' at the Savoy	F	Benny Goodman, Webb & Sampson	Robbins	1936
All God's children got rhythm	F	Kaper & Jurman	Francis Day & Hunter	1937
Cherokee	B♭	Ray Noble	Peter Maurice	1938
Spring is here	A♭	Richard Rodgers	Francis, Day & Hunter	1938
I didn't know what time it was	G	Richard Rodgers	Chappell	1939
All the things you are	A♭	Jerome Kern	Chappell	1940
Perdido	B♭	Juan Tizol	Campbell Connelly	1942
Thing's ain't wot they used to be	E♭	Mercer Ellington	Campbell Connelly	1943
I'll remember April	G	Raye, de Paul & Johnston	Leeds	1951
Django	Fm	John Lewis	Kensington	1955
Graas Point	C	Johnny Graas	Champion	1955

Appendix B: Records

1. *Records referred to in the text (marked *)*

'Take this hammer' (p.) 46 Rock Island Line	RCA	RCX–146	7″
'Panama' (p. 18) Kid Ory, Vol. 2	Good Time Jazz	EPG 1171	7″
'Dippermouth Blues' (p. 55) King Oliver's Creole Jazz Band 1923	Riverside	RLP 8805	12″
'Cornet Chop Suey' (p. 56) His Greatest Years, No. 1	Parlophone	PMC 1140	12″
'Honky Tonk Train Blues' (p. 59) Honky Tonk Train	Riverside	RLP 8806	12″

'East St. Louis Toodle-oo'
   (p. 65)
The Ellington Era 1927–40,
   Vol. 1, Part 1
	CBS	BPG 62178	12″

'All the things you are' (p. 69) Bird of Paradise	Allegro	ALL 798	12″

'Stompin' at the Savoy' (p. 75)
The Great Dizzy Gillespie,
   Charlie Christian & Thelonius
   Monk
	Society	SOC 996	12″

'Anthropology' (p. 71) The Greatest of Dizzy Gillespie	RCA	RV 27242	12″
'Django' (p. 14) The Best of the Modern Jazz Quartet	Stateside	SL 10141	12″

Note: These are 'anthology' pieces and so are likely to be always available. But the particular anthology they are in may change from time to time.

2.   *Recorded artists representative of different jazz styles*

PRE-JAZZ ERA
Work Songs. Huddie Ledbetter (Leadbelly).
Country Blues. Sleepy John Estes, Robert Johnson.
Gospel Songs and Spirituals. Mahalia Jackson, Rosetta Tharpe, The Staple Singers.
Classic Women's Blues. Ma Rainey, Bessie Smith.
City Blues. Muddy Waters, Big Maceo Merriwether.

RAGTIME AND EARLY JAZZ
Ragtime Piano. Pianola recordings (Scott Joplin and others), Jelly Roll Morton.
New Orleans Jazz. Kid Ory (tbn.), King Oliver (tpt.).

1920s CHICAGO
Negro: Louis Armstrong (tpt.), Johnny Dodds (clt.).
White: Bix Beiderbecke (tpt.), Frank Teschemacher (clt.).
Boogie-Woogie Piano: Jimmy Yancey, Pinetop Smith.

1930s SWING
Big Bands: Fletcher Henderson, Luis Russell (arrangers); Duke Ellington, Count Basie (pno./leaders); Benny Goodman (clt./leader), Artie Shaw (clt./leader).
Small jam bands: Fats Waller (pno.), Teddy Wilson (pno.).
Tenor saxes: Coleman Hawkins, Lester Young.

1940s NEW INSPIRATIONS: BEBOP
Charlie Parker (alto sax.), Dizzy Gillespie (tpt.), Thelonius Monk (pno.), Bud Powell (pno.), Charlie Christian (gtr.), Woody Herman big band. Dizzy Gillespie Afro-Cuban numbers (1947).

1950s COOL AND WEST COAST JAZZ
Miles Davis 9-piece group, Bud Shank (flute), Dave Brubeck (pno.), Shorty Rogers (tpt.), Gerry Mulligan (baritone sax.), Stan Kenton Orchestra.

1950s EAST COAST
Modern Jazz Quartet, Miles Davis (tpt.), Clifford Brown (tpt.), Art Blakey (drums), Sonny Rollins (tenor sax.).

JAZZ IN EUROPE
Humphrey Lyttleton (tpt.) England, John Dankworth (alto sax.)
England, Bengt Hallberg (pno.) Sweden, Arne Domnerus (alto sax.)
Sweden, Sven Asmussen (vln.) Denmark, Martial Solal (pno.)
France, Bernard Peiffer (pno.) France.

1960s NEW WAVE
John Coltrane (tenor sax.), Eric Dolphy (alto sax.), Charles Mingus
(bass), Ornette Coleman (alto sax.).

Appendix C: Books on Jazz

To select a limited number of books for further reading is an extremely difficult task; however, there are four which stand out for me as being very useful general surveys. The first is *Jazz* by Rex Harris (Pelican, 1952) an excellent book for tracing the background and early history of jazz up to the 1930s. The second is a comprehensive study of the modern jazz scene: *Modern Jazz: A survey of developments since 1939* by Morgan and Horricks (Gollancz, 1956). For very studious readers there is a book by Leroy Ostransky, entitled *The Anatomy of Jazz* (University of Washington Press). Lastly, Gunther Schuller's *Early Jazz—Its Roots and Musical Development* (Oxford University Press, 1968) is a large-scale study of the musical character of jazz.

INDEX OF TECHNICAL TERMS,
STYLES, ETC.

INDEX OF JAZZ MUSICIANS

Set by William Clowes & Sons Ltd
& reprinted lithographically by
Clarke Doble & Brendon Ltd., Plymouth

6103